EYE ON ENERGY

Fossil Fuels

ABDO
Publishing Company

Jill C. Wheeler

visit us at
www.abdopublishing.com

Published by ABDO Publishing Company, 8000 West 78th Street, Edina, Minnesota 55439. Copyright © 2008 by Abdo Consulting Group, Inc. International copyrights reserved in all countries. No part of this book may be reproduced in any form without written permission from the publisher. The Checkerboard Library™ is a trademark and logo of ABDO Publishing Company.

Printed in the United States.

Cover Photo: Corbis
Interior Photos: Alamy pp. 7, 14, 23, 27; AP Images pp. 11, 13, 17, 25; Corbis pp. 5, 8, 15, 18; Getty Images pp. 9, 10, 16, 20, 21, 22; North Wind p. 4; Peter Arnold p. 29

Series Coordinator: Rochelle Baltzer
Editors: Rochelle Baltzer, BreAnn Rumsch
Art Direction & Cover Design: Neil Klinepier

Library of Congress Cataloging-in-Publication Data

Wheeler, Jill C., 1964-
 Fossil fuels / Jill C. Wheeler.
   p. cm. – (Eye on energy)
 Includes index.
 ISBN 978–1–59928–805–5
 1. Fossil fuels–Juvenile literature. I. Title.

TP318.3.W54 2008
333.8'2–dc22

2007007109

CONTENTS

IT'S ELECTRIFYING

Electricity is a major part of our lifestyle. It allows us to be more comfortable, productive, and entertained. Just think about an average day. Electricity powers your alarm clock every morning. It keeps the lights on at your school. Electricity is also at work when you watch television or check your e-mail.

The Pearl Street Station used coal energy to power newly invented electric lightbulbs.

The first electricity-generating station in the United States opened in 1882 in New York City, New York. The Pearl Street Station originally supplied electricity to just 59 customers. Soon, the electricity industry took off. In 1907, 8 percent of U.S. homes used electricity. That amount increased to 67 percent by 1932.

So, where does all of that electricity come from? Today, about 66 percent of electricity in the United States is produced from burning fossil fuels. The most important fossil fuels are oil, coal, and natural gas. When burned, these fuels have incredible energy **potential**. And, they are generally less expensive than other energy sources.

However, there are downsides to this type of energy. Burning fossil fuels **emits** gases that cause pollution and contribute to global warming. And, some fossil fuels are located in politically unstable parts of the world. So, the United States may not always have access to these resources.

FOSSILS TO ENERGY

Fossil fuels currently supply 85 percent of the world's energy demands. Fossil fuels are hydrocarbons. Hydrocarbons are chemicals that contain just two **elements**, carbon and hydrogen. Because this combination burns easily, fossil fuels make powerful energy sources.

Carbon is found in all living things, including humans. It is recycled into the atmosphere when living things breathe. It is also recycled in this way when they die. Fossil fuels contain carbon from ancient living things. That carbon is returned to the atmosphere when fossil fuels are burned.

Most of the world's fossil fuels were formed about 300 million years ago. At that time, the earth looked very different. The land was covered with swamps containing trees and large, leafy plants. The seas were filled with algae (AL-jee). Prehistoric animals, sea creatures, and plants lived in these places. After dying, they sank to the bottom of these swamps and seas.

Various processes are used to mine fossil fuels. When coal appears in deposits near Earth's surface, such as this line of coal, workers often use surface-mining methods.

Over time, sand, clay, and minerals settled on top of the plant and animal remains. These materials slowly turned into **sedimentary** rock. As rock layers settled over the remains, heat and pressure increased. Millions of years passed, and the squeezed remains slowly formed oil, coal, or natural gas.

OIL

Most people think of oil when they think about fossil fuels. Petroleum, or crude oil, is the leading fossil fuel. It supplies 40 percent of the world's energy. However, some scientists believe that petroleum will be gone in 60 to 70 years if the world keeps using it at the current rate.

Petroleum is a thick, dark-colored liquid found in certain rock formations. To obtain it, workers drill a well to a deposit. The well acts as a passageway for the oil to flow to the surface. Once **extracted**, the oil travels through pipelines or on ships to a **refinery**. At a refinery, it is processed into a usable form.

Pump systems create suction to draw up oil from wells.

Most petroleum is refined to make fuel. Gasoline, diesel fuel, jet fuel, and heating fuel are all made from petroleum. Some petroleum is converted into petrochemicals to make products including plastics, fertilizers, and cosmetics.

At an oil refinery, oil travels through towers, tanks, and pipes. It is separated, converted, and chemically treated to become a useful product.

Humans began using petroleum more than 5,000 years ago. Ancient Egyptians first used it for medicines. Oil was also used to make weapons during ancient times. In the United States, oil was first successfully drilled in 1859 in Pennsylvania. By the end of the 1800s, oil fields had been discovered in 14 states.

The United States was the world's leading oil producer until the 1940s. Today, the United States only controls about 3 percent of the world's petroleum reserves. Yet it uses about 25 percent. That means most of the country's oil is imported. A majority of it comes from Canada, Mexico, and Saudi Arabia.

The first oil well in Titusville, Pennsylvania, laid the foundation for the petroleum industry in the United States.

Oil has changed the way Americans live and work. It has helped the country succeed. Yet, oil has drawbacks. Drilling for oil and transporting it can cause pollution if the oil leaks or spills. And, burning gasoline and diesel fuel **emits** pollutants and **greenhouse gases**. These emissions can cause smog and **acid rain**. They also **intensify** global warming.

In addition to **environmental** sacrifices, there are political challenges that accompany obtaining oil. Most of the world's wealthiest countries use more petroleum than they produce. Some poorer countries produce more petroleum than they use. Wealthy countries importing large amounts of petroleum can lead to global problems, including war.

The Trans-Alaska Pipeline System (TAPS) is one of the world's largest pipeline systems, running for 800 miles (1,290 km). TAPS carries oil from Prudhoe Bay in Alaska to North America's northernmost ice-free port, Valdez, Alaska.

OIL FROM SAND

Much of the world's oil is locked in rock formations. One of these oil-rich formations is the Athabasca tar sands of Alberta, Canada. Geologists say that these tar sands might have more oil than Saudi Arabia.

In tar sands, oil is contained in **bitumen** (buh-TYOO-muhn) rock. Oil in bitumen is a semisolid form of petroleum. New technologies allow companies to remove this nonliquid oil from its rocky home.

One method for removing oil from deep underground reserves involves multidirectional wells. Two wells now take the place of what once required many individual wells. Steam is **injected** into one well to melt oil. Then, the oil is pumped out of the other well.

For oil that lies at the earth's surface, another method can be used. Huge trucks strip-mine loads of tar sand. The loads are dumped into a heated mixer that separates bitumen from the sand.

It is more difficult and costly to obtain nonliquid oil. Both of these methods require many workers. In addition, they burn a lot of fossil fuels.

Workers operate heavy machinery when strip-mining the Athabasca tar sands.
This truck is 17 feet (5 m) tall and 32 feet (10 m) long, with 12-foot (4-m) tires!

COAL

Coal is the most plentiful fossil fuel. It supplies 24 percent of the world's energy. At the present rate of use, the world's coal supply can last for several hundred more years. However, burning coal is also a major cause of pollution.

Coal is a black- or brown-colored solid that is found in **sedimentary** deposits. It can be mined from the earth's surface or from underground. To mine from the surface, rock and soil layers must be removed. Then, coal is dug up and transported. Underground mining requires tunneling deep beneath the surface to coal deposits.

In the United States, coal is primarily used for electricity. But in parts of Asia and Europe, it is commonly used to heat buildings and homes. Many manufacturing substances are also made from coal. Of these substances, coke is the most widely used. Coke is mainly used to make iron and steel. Some waste products from coal are used to make asphalt, cement, and concrete.

The average American uses about 20 pounds (9 kg) of coal each day! Turning on a light or charging a computer may use coal.

A coal power plant that supplies the electricity needs of 500,000 homes produces the same amount of harmful emissions per year as 750,000 cars.

The Chinese were the first to develop a coal industry. They were mining coal from the earth's surface by AD 300. In the United States, the first commercial coal mine opened in 1748 near Richmond, Virginia. Coal was originally mined by hand. Mining machines were introduced in the 1880s and are still used today.

Coal quickly became a favorite energy source. Today, it produces more than half of the electricity used in the United States. Luckily, the U.S. coal supply is plentiful. Scientists estimate U.S. coal reserves contain more than three times the energy of Saudi Arabia's oil reserves. This abundance makes coal-produced electricity relatively inexpensive.

Coal miners have a dangerous yet important job.

However, critics say coal has greater costs than most people think. Burning it creates more **greenhouse gases** than burning other fuels. It also **emits** other pollutants that are key factors in **acid rain** and smog. These pollutants can contribute to heart problems and **respiratory** illnesses.

A specialist tests water in southeast Ohio, where abandoned coal mines have caused high pollution levels. Ohio must clean more than 1,000 miles (1,600 km) of polluted streams.

Mining coal has serious costs, too. Underground coal mining is especially risky. The process has become safer over time. However, mining accidents still claim hundreds of lives each year.

Coal mining can also change the landscape surrounding the mine. Sometimes, trees must be removed. Local water sources can become polluted, too. Preparing coal for burning can also lead to water **contamination**. Finally, transporting coal by train releases pollutants into the air.

NEW TECHNOLOGIES

Coal travels through many pipelines at an IGCC plant.

New technologies take advantage of the coal supply in the United States. The integrated gasification combined cycle (IGCC) and the Fischer-Tropsch process turn coal into other products.

The IGCC process turns coal into gas. Burning gas produces less harmful **emissions** than burning coal. IGCC plants are also about 10 percent more **efficient** than standard coal plants. They are estimated to use 40 percent less water and produce half as much solid waste. However, IGCC plants are more costly to build than standard coal plants.

The Fischer-Tropsch process turns coal into diesel fuel. It can also convert coal into natural gas. Even crop wastes and wood chips can be turned into fuels using this process.

Some people believe that using the Fischer-Tropsch process would help reduce the United States' dependence on foreign oil. However, the process emits **greenhouse gases**. In fact, **refining** coal can release 50 to 100 percent more **carbon dioxide** than refining petroleum.

PROJECT SPOTLIGHT

MESABA ENERGY PROJECT

Plans are in progress in Taconite, Minnesota, to build the first large-scale coal-gasification electric power plant in the United States. Construction is set to begin in 2008. The Mesaba Energy Project is expected to spark more interest in coal-gasification technology.

ENERGY CAPACITY: The plant will generate 606 megawatts per unit, which is planned to supply electricity to about 600,000 Minnesota homes

TIMELINE: The plant is expected to begin generating electricity in late 2011.

FUEL: The plant will use coal or coal-blends as fuel.

PROCESS: Fuel is crushed and mixed with water. Then, it is pumped into a pressurized container called a gasifier along with purified oxygen. In the gasifier, controlled reactions convert the fuel into syngas. The syngas is burned to produce electricity.

HIGHLIGHTS: The IGCC process to be used in the plant is estimated to reduce pollution by 60 percent, compared with traditional coal-fired power plants. The Mesaba Energy Project will be the cleanest coal-fired power plant in the world!

The Mesaba Energy Project will bring many jobs to Taconite, Minnesota, once construction and operations begin.

NATURAL GAS

Natural gas is the least used fossil fuel. It supplies 22 percent of the world's energy needs. Yet, natural gas has many perks. It is easily transported through pipelines. It also burns cleaner than other fossil fuels. Generating electricity from natural gas **emits** just 40 percent of the **carbon dioxide** produced by coal-generated electricity.

Natural gas is made up mostly of methane. Methane is a colorless and odorless gas. It is also highly flammable and weighs less than air. Most natural gas can be found near oil reserves. Often, oil and gas flow to the surface from the same underground formation.

Like oil, natural gas is most commonly pumped from the ground. Then, it travels through pipelines to where it is needed. Yet some natural gas flows freely to wells, which require only surface pipes and valves. These pipes direct gas to its end point.

Natural gas is delivered to Americans through a 1.3 million-mile (2.1 million-km) network of underground pipes. Stretched out, those pipes would reach to the moon and back twice!

Natural gas is commonly used to heat homes and offices. In homes, it often powers cooking and heating appliances. However, natural gas can be deadly if it leaks. For that reason, gas companies add a smelly chemical to it so that people will realize if there is a leak. If you smell a rotten-egg odor in your home, go outside right away. Then, ask a neighbor to call the police.

Flames on a gas-burning stove should always be blue. If they are yellow, the gas might be emitting harmful fumes. In that case, the stove should be checked promptly by a professional.

When natural gas lamps were widely used, some people worked as lamplighters. They lit and unlit streetlights. Sometimes, lamplighters also acted as town watchmen.

Humans discovered natural gas in Iran between 6000 and 2000 BC. People noticed fires that kept burning, yet they did not see any fuel. The gas was naturally seeping out of the ground. Most likely, lightning started the fires and the gas kept them burning.

In the United States, natural gas was first used as fuel in 1816. It powered streetlamps in Baltimore, Maryland. The first well in the country to **extract** natural gas was dug in Fredonia, New York, in 1821. Throughout most of the 1800s, natural gas was used almost solely as lamp fuel. Very few gas pipelines were built until after the 1940s.

Today, natural gas generates about 15 percent of the electricity in the United States. Like other fossil fuels, natural gas has drawbacks. Much of it is located in **environmentally** sensitive areas. In the United States, these places include coastlines and parts of the Rocky Mountains. Some methods of obtaining natural gas can damage land and **contaminate** nearby water supplies.

The first offshore natural gas well completely out of sight from land was drilled in 1947 in the Gulf of Mexico. Today, about 25 percent of the natural gas produced in the United States comes from offshore drilling.

LNG

One alternative to drilling for natural gas in sensitive areas is to import it. Transporting gas in its natural state would be difficult. Yet, there is a technology that has made importing gas a reality.

In the late 1800s, scientists discovered they could turn natural gas into a liquid by chilling it. The result is called liquefied natural gas (LNG). The process was once very expensive. However, LNG technology has been improved, making the process less costly.

At -259 degrees Fahrenheit (-162°C), natural gas becomes a liquid. It also shrinks. The natural gas that would fit inside a beach ball at room temperature would fit inside a Ping-Pong ball at -259 degrees Fahrenheit. This makes it easier to transport on tankers.

After LNG arrives, it is warmed until it becomes a gas again. Then it is pumped into existing gas pipelines. However, finding a safe place for a tanker to unload can be difficult.

If the gas inside a tanker were ever **ignited**, there would be a terrible fire. So, tankers unload at ports far from large cities. Because of **environmental** concerns, it can take many years to approve construction for a new port.

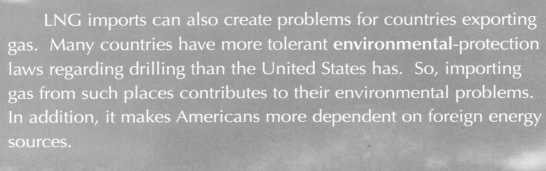

LNG imports can also create problems for countries exporting gas. Many countries have more tolerant **environmental**-protection laws regarding drilling than the United States has. So, importing gas from such places contributes to their environmental problems. In addition, it makes Americans more dependent on foreign energy sources.

Gas-rich places such as Algeria, Trinidad, and Nigeria export LNG to the United States on tankers. These giant ships can be up to 1,000 feet (300 m) long!

GLOBAL WARMING

Earth's atmosphere lets most of the sun's light pass through to the surface. As the sunlight heats Earth's surface, part of that energy is sent back toward space as **radiation**. On its way through the atmosphere, **greenhouse gases** absorb some of the radiation. This heats the atmosphere, which heats Earth's surface. This natural process is called the greenhouse effect.

Global warming refers to an increase in the Earth's average surface temperature. This increase is because the greenhouse effect has **intensified** since the late 1800s. Many scientists believe this is due to human activity. For example, burning fossil fuels is a leading greenhouse gas contributor.

Scientists worry that people and nature might not adapt to rapid climate changes. So, they suggest cutting the world's greenhouse gas **emissions**. They estimate emissions must be reduced 50 to 70 percent by 2050.

FACT OR FICTION?

Over the past 100 years, the earth's surface temperature has decreased an average of 1.1 degrees Fahrenheit (0.6°C).

Fiction. It has actually increased 1.1 degrees Fahrenheit (0.6°C). Scientists conclude that this temperature increase was probably the largest in the past 1,000 years.

If **emissions** are not cut, scientists believe there may be grave consequences. Polar ice caps could melt. This would cause sea levels to rise, changing coastlines worldwide. Global warming could also cause severe weather patterns, reduce crop yields, and harm plants and animals.

The United States has nearly 4.6 percent of the world's population. However, it produces about 25 percent of the world's greenhouse gases. Transportation is one of the main greenhouse gas contributors.

KYOTO PROTOCOL

The Kyoto Protocol is an international effort to reduce greenhouse gas emissions by 2012. It went into effect in February 2005. The treaty restricts the amount of emissions for developed countries that have signed the agreement.

Countries can take actions to earn credits that reduce the amount of emissions they must cut. They can plant forests, which absorb carbon dioxide. They can also invest in building cleaner power plants in developing countries.

The protocol does not require developing countries to limit emissions. Those countries contribute the least to global warming. However, developing countries can receive economic aid in exchange for reducing emissions.

In the Future

Fossil fuels have enormous energy **potential**. Many are still in good supply. Yet now more than ever, using them depends on the ability to reduce their **greenhouse gas emissions**.

Global warming concerns have researchers studying ways to store greenhouse gases. Burying **carbon dioxide** is one plan. Some carbon dioxide is already pumped into the ground to help **extract** oil. Some scientists say that it can also be stored in deep saltwater **aquifers** (A-kwuh-fuhrz).

However, not all regions of the world have access to such sites. Plus, **injecting** carbon dioxide into the ground can set off earthquakes. Transporting carbon dioxide is difficult, too. So far, direct pipelines from power plants to storage sites do not exist.

Dangers of storing carbon dioxide underground have also been proven by nature. In 1986, about 1,700 people died when a natural carbon dioxide deposit suddenly rose to the surface of a lake in Cameroon, Africa. Some people fear this could happen again if a large amount of carbon dioxide stored underground were to escape.

As with all energy sources, there are both benefits and drawbacks to using fossil fuel power. Fossil fuel energy continues to be discussed. Scientists will further study its **environmental** toll. Yet it is also important to be responsible about using power. Do what you can to conserve Earth's energy sources so they last for years to come!

Riding a bicycle instead of riding in a car helps limit the amount of greenhouse gases released into the atmosphere.

FIVE SIMPLE WAYS TO SAVE ENERGY

1. Use fluorescent lightbulbs instead of standard lightbulbs.

2. Turn off lights when you leave a room. Also, turn off televisions, radios, and computers when they aren't in use.

3. Instead of using a store's paper or plastic bags, bring cloth bags with you when you shop.

4. If you are going somewhere nearby, walk or ride your bicycle instead of riding in a car.

5. Recycle! Contact your recycling service to find out what items can be recycled.

GLOSSARY

acid rain - rain, sleet, or snow that contains high amounts of acid-forming chemicals. The burning of coal, gasoline, and oil largely contribute to the formation of acid rain.

aquifer - a layer of rock, sand, or gravel that can absorb water.

bitumen - a light brown to black solid or semisolid consisting mainly of hydrocarbons. Bitumen naturally occurs as asphalt and as a thick crude oil.

carbon dioxide - a heavy, fireproof, colorless gas that is formed when fuel containing the element carbon is burned.

contaminate - to make unfit for use by adding something harmful or unpleasant.

efficient - the ability to produce a desired result, especially without wasting time or energy.

element - any of the more than 100 basic substances that have atoms of only one kind.

emit - to give off or out. An emission is something that has been emitted.

environmental - of or having to do with all the surroundings that affect the growth and well-being of a living thing.

extract - to withdraw by a physical or chemical process.

greenhouse gas - a gas, such as carbon dioxide, that traps heat in the atmosphere.

ignite - to set on fire.

inject - to drive or force into something.

intensify - to make something exist in a more extreme degree.

potential - capable of being or becoming. Something that is possible, but not actual.

radiation - the transfer of heat through matter or space in the form of waves or particles.

refine - to purify. A refinery is the building and the machinery for purifying products, such as petroleum.

respiratory - having to do with the system of organs involved with breathing.

sedimentary - of, relating to, or containing sediment. Sediment is fine sand, clay, or soil carried by water that settles on the bottom of rivers, lakes, swamps, and oceans.

WEB SITES

To learn more about fossil fuels, visit ABDO Publishing Company on the World Wide Web at **www.abdopublishing.com**. Web sites about fossil fuels are featured on our Book Links page. These links are routinely monitored and updated to provide the most current information available.

INDEX